To Anna and Owen – C.L.
For Todd and all his friends in Miss Perryman's class – A.W.

First published as 'Paint a Sun in the Sky'
in Great Britain in 1999 by Macdonald Young Books

This edition published in 2009 by Wayland,
an imprint of Hachette Children's Books,
338 Euston Road, London NW1 3BH
www.hachettelivre.co.uk

Commissioning Editor Dereen Taylor
Editor Rosie Nixon
Designer Liz Black
Science and Language Consultant Dr Carol Ballard

Claire Llewellyn
A Picture of the year: A first look at seasons.
(Little Bees)
1. Seasons - Juvenile Literature
I. Titlell Wood, Amanda
508.2

Printed in China by WKT Co. Ltd.

ISBN 978 0 7502 5844 9

A Picture of the Year

A Picture of the Year

by Claire Llewellyn
Illustrated by Amanda Wood

WAYLAND

Spring blossom opens, and flowers

shoot up through the chilly ground.

11

In summer, the sun is high in the sky.

Out go thick jumpers and heavy coats.

In come sunhats, T-shirts and shorts.

13

Flowerbeds and windowboxes buzz with bees.

Bees use nectar to make honey.

Butterflies flutter through the air.

And I can see a butterfly drinking nectar from a flower.

15

Soon, the leaves on the trees change colour

and blow away in the wind.

Did you see that squirrel?

I bet it's hiding food for the winter.

In winter, the sun is low in the sky.

The days are short and cold.

The best winter days have

bright sunshine and snow.

all winter long. They'll wake up again in the spring.

That squirrel looks
warm and cosy!

make up a picture of the year.

...a sun in the sky!

29

Why do we have seasons?

We have seasons because of the way the Earth moves around the Sun. This journey is called the Earth's orbit and it takes exactly one year.

1 In December, the South Pole leans towards the Sun. The south has summer. The north has winter.

The Earth isn't upright as it orbits the Sun. It's tilted to one side. So, at different times on its journey, first one pole and then the other leans towards the Sun. This is why we have seasons.

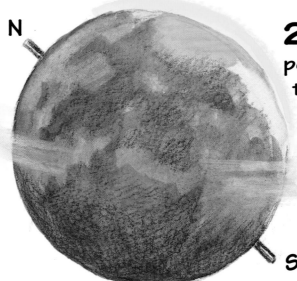

2 In March, neither pole leans towards the Sun, but the south is getting cooler (autumn) and the north is warming up (spring).

4 In September, neither pole leans towards the Sun, but it's getting warmer in the south (spring) and cooler in the north (autumn).

S

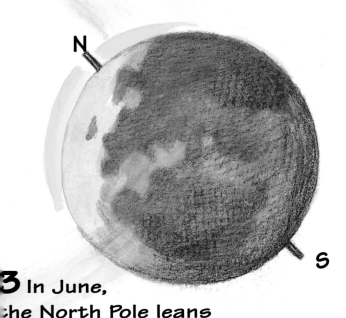

N

S

3 In June, the North Pole leans towards the Sun. The north has summer. The south has winter.

Useful words

Blossom
Small flowers that open on trees in spring.

Nectar
The sweet juice inside a flower.

Orbit
The pathway of the Earth as it moves around the Sun.

Pole
The name given to the most northern and most southern parts of the Earth.

Season
A part of the year that has its own sort of weather.